A New True Book

ROBOTS

By Carol Greene

This "true book" was prepared
under the direction of
Illa Podendorf,
formerly with the Laboratory School,
University of Chicago

 CHILDRENS PRESS™

CHICAGO

Toy robots on parade

PHOTO CREDITS

©Ray Hillstrom—Cover

Wide World Photo—2, 24, 25 (2 photos), 32, 36 (2 photos) 41

National Aeronautics and Space Administration—26, 27, 34, 38, 40

Creative Systems—4, 31 (2 photos)

Argonne National Laboratory—35, 43

Marty Hansen—6

Cincinnati Milacron—8, 28

Historical Pictures Services, Chicago—9, 11, 13, 15 (2 photos), 16, 17

Westinghouse Electric Corporation—19

General Electric: Research and Development Center—22, 29;
    Manmate Manipulator Products—20, 33

Margaret Cooper—39 (2 photos)

Root Resources—Earl L. Kubis, 44

Library of Congress Cataloging in Publication Data

Greene, Carol.
    Robots.

    (A New true book)
    Includes index.
    Summary: Briefly discusses the history and uses of automatically opening devices from mechanical toys through dishwashers and clock radios to cyborgs and manipulators.
    1. Automata—Juvenile literature. 2. Robots, industrial—Juvenile literature. [1. Automata.
2. Robots] I. Title
TJ211.G73   1983   629.8'92   82-17872
ISBN 0-516-01684-9   AACR2

TABLE OF CONTENTS

Robots promoting products always attract a crowd.

WHAT IS A ROBOT?

Have you ever used a robot? Think a minute before you answer. What *is* a robot?

A robot is any machine that can do work without a person running it all the time.

That means an automatic washer is a robot. It can switch from wash to rinse to spin dry all by itself. A dishwasher is a robot, too. So is a clock radio.

Well, what do you know? You've used lots of robots. They may not look

In many ways, an automatic dishwasher is a robot.

like the robots in movies.
But they are robots all the
same.

Karel Čapek made up
the word *robot* in the
1920s. He was from
Czechoslovakia and he
wrote a play called *R.U.R.*
(That stands for Rossum's
Universal Robots.) Robot
comes from the Czech
word for "to work." In
Čapek's play, a man has a
factory run by robots. He's

a mean man and one day
the robots take over.

But the *idea* of robots
was around long before
Čapek invented the word.
The idea of robots goes
back thousands of years.

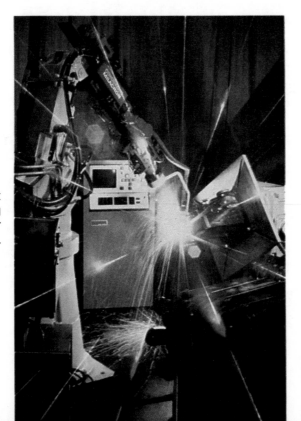

This robot
is building
an arm for
another robot.

FROM TOYS TO THINKERS

The first robots were mostly toys for grown-ups. People enjoyed them. But they didn't take them too seriously.

This ancient Greek toy worked automatically. When the apple was picked up, the archer, Hercules, shot his arrow and the dragon hissed.

About 3,400 years ago, the Egyptians had human figures on their clocks. These figures could ring bells to tell the time. They were run by waterpower.

Over a thousand years later, a Greek named Archytas supposedly made a wooden pigeon that could fly.

Mechanical singing birds have been built for hundreds of years.

Another thousand years
later, Emperor Constantine VII
of Byzantium had a tree
full of mechanical birds.
They could flap their wings
and sing.

11

In the 1200s, a man called Albertus Magnus invented a type of robot. Some stories say it could walk. Others say it could talk, too.

An English scientist, Roger Bacon, also built a robot in the 1200s. He hoped it would tell him the secrets of the universe. Smoke poured from this robot. Its eyes glowed. Its jaw even moved. But it didn't tell Bacon any secrets.

Over the years, many people made mechanical figures. Most were toys.

This automatic toy was called the Fiddling Ape.

Then, in the 1700s,
people began to learn
more about machines.
James Watt invented the
steam engine. Soon
factories were using more
and more machines. During
the 1800s and 1900s,
Thomas Edison discovered
ways of using electricity.

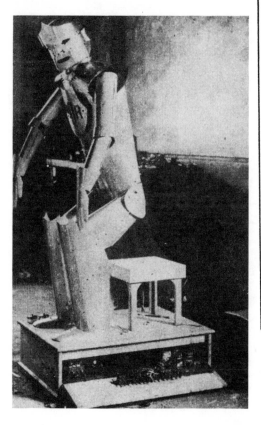

A robot (left) sits down after giving
a speech. Edison's talking doll
was sold in 1890.

By the 1930s, people
knew a lot about
machines. They had many
kinds of machines. They
were ready to take robots
seriously.

15

Alpha was programmed to do many different things.

In 1932, a robot called Alpha was shown in London. It could read, bow, tell time, sing, and smoke cigars.

Elektro and his dog Sparky were big hits at the

This electric dog was designed to follow light.

New York World's Fair in 1939. Elektro could walk and count on his fingers. He could give Sparky orders. And he could obey spoken orders himself. Sparky could wag his tail and bark.

In 1948, William Gray Walter built two robot turtles, Elmer and Elsie. They could move around without bumping into things. In 1952, Claude Shannon built a robot mouse. It could find its way through a maze. These were robots that could *think*—at least a little.

A robot welds metal.

Many people thought
these robots were still toys.
But scientists knew better.
They knew the time for
robots had come. So they
got busy.

Designed to work underwater, this robot manipulator
can dive deeper and stay longer underwater than
human divers can. But like all manipulators, it needs
a human operator to function.

Finally, in the late 1950s, the Mobots were born. A Mobot is a mobile robot—a robot that can move or be moved. Soon Mobots were working in factories, labs, and even under the ocean.

At the same time, scientists were working hard on computers. They knew computers would be important for the future of robots. They were right.

A TV camera acts as eyes for this robot assembler.

BOXES AND BUGS

If someone asked you to draw a picture of a robot, how would it look? Like a person? That's how we often picture robots in our minds. But real robots look many different ways.

Some robots have TV cameras for eyes. Some have special cells that help them touch. Many have computer brains. How robots look depends on the job they have to do. Some can even have their parts changed so they can do different jobs.

This robot has been designed to do housework.

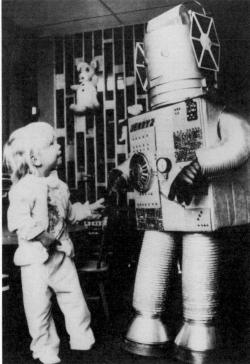

Above: Operated by remote control this robot has been built to look for and identify a bomb.

Left: A robot, named Jerry 2, visited hospitals and raised money for the March of Dimes.

Interior view of the Viking Lander Capsule that landed on Mars.

Some robots look like huge bugs. NASA sent these Viking Landers to Mars in 1976. They moved around on the surface, picked up soil, and did experiments.

The Viking Lander Capsule separates from its spacecraft.

Industrial robots spot weld automobile bodies on an assembly line.

Robots can do boring jobs. They can do dangerous jobs with fast-moving machinery. They can do messy jobs, such as spray painting. They can do jobs no person could do, such as picking up hot metal.

A robot can be programmed to assemble a wide variety of products.

Robots don't get bored. They don't get tired. They don't mind getting messy.

Some people are afraid robots will take jobs away from people. But that doesn't have to happen. After all, people are in charge of robots. People must remember that robots are good at some things and humans are good at others.

Some robots go around
telling people that they
don't have to be afraid of
robots. These robots help
people understand that
robots can do dull, nasty
jobs so people can do
better ones.

ROBOTS' RELATIVES

What would you call a creature who was part robot, part human? Some people call these creatures *cyborgs*.

This robot can bend at the hip, knee, and ankle.

Hardiman is a metal skeleton. The demonstrator is attached at the feet, waist, and hands. Wearing Hardiman he can pick up 1,500 pounds.

Medical scientists are working on cyborgs, too. They hope that an outside skeleton will one day help some disabled people walk by themselves.

The space shutle has a manipulator arm.

Manipulators are a little like cyborgs. They work with people. A scientist who uses mechanical hands to pick up radioactive materials is using a manipulator.

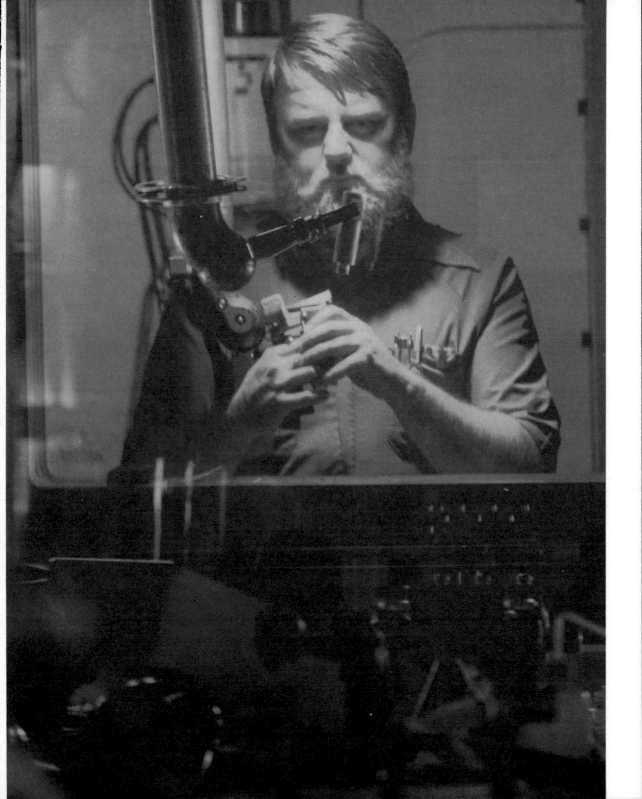

Because they are machines, robots are being built to do jobs that could be dangerous to humans. For example the robot tank (below) could be used to handle radioactive materials.

Some big manipulators are sent miles under the sea. No person could go that deep.

Other manipulators are sent into dangerous situations. People control where they go and what they pick up by remote control.

Astronauts train in simulators that are built to give them experience with conditions they will find in outer space.

Simulators are robots' relatives, too. They often look like people. Simulators are used to test cars in crashes. They are used to test conditions in outer space.

Medical students practice on them. These simulators can bleed and get bruises. Some even turn blue if the student makes a mistake!

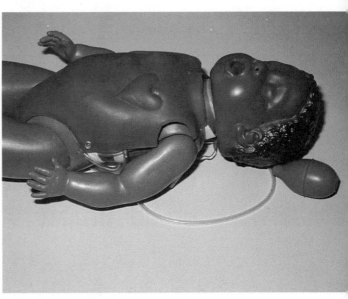

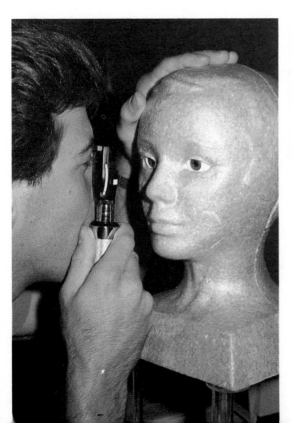

The simulator at left gives students experience examining the eye. The one above is used to provide students practice giving mouth-to-mouth respiration to an infant.

IF YOU HAD A ROBOT

If you had a robot, what
could he do? Well, he
could empty your garbage
and walk your dog. But
you'd spend a lot of time
programming him to do

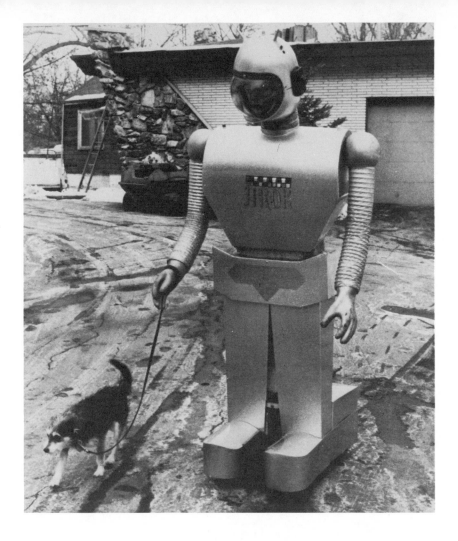

these things. You'd have to
be sure he knew the
difference between your
garbage and your dog!

As computers get better and better, so will robots.

Robots are working all over the world. Mini-robots in England make watches. A factory in Japan uses all robot workers. The Soviet Union uses robots, too. There are factories that make robots.

Robots can do human jobs. But they are not like humans. They are

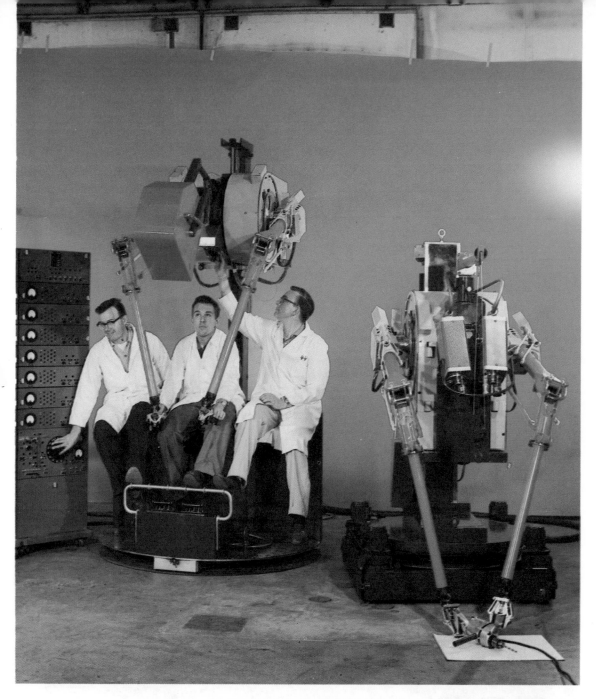

A slave-robot designed to repair or handle highly radioactive materials. The men at left run the robot by remote control. On a TV screen they can see what the robot's (right) two TV cameras see.

machines. They don't have feelings. They don't have an imagination. So far, they can't make new robots.

Robots can be a lot of fun. They can do jobs that make life better for people. But they can't take the place of people. They can't be human. It's important for the people who use robots to remember that!

WORDS YOU SHOULD KNOW

Archytas (ar • KIE • tus) — the name of a Greek person who is said to have made a wooden bird that could fly

automatic (auto • MAT • ik) — working, moving, or acting by itself

bored (BORD) — to become tired because something is dull or uninteresting

cyborg (SYE • borg) — something that is part robot and part human

Czechoslovakia (Check • us • low • VAK • ee • ah) — a country in Europe

disabled (dis • ABE • ild) — not able; crippled

Emperor Constantine (EM • per • er KAHN • stan • teen) — a ruler of Byzantium who lived long ago

invent (in • VENT) — to make something new

manipulator (man • IP • you • lay • ter) — something that can handle or move something else

maze (MAIZ) — a winding pattern of paths through which it is hard to find the way

mechanical (mih • KAN • ih • kil) — of or using machines or tools

mobile (MOH • bill) — able to move or be moved from place to place

radioactive (ray • dee • oh • ACT • iv) — able to give off energy in the form of certain kinds of rays

robot (ROH • bot) — a machine that does work without a person running it all the time

serious (SEER • ee • us) — important; not smiling or joking

simulator (SIM • you • lay • tor) — something that pretends to be something else

specimen (SPESS • ih • men) — a sample

universe (YOO • nih • verss) — everything that is; earth, planets, and space

INDEX

About the Author

Carol Greene has written over 25 books for children, plus stories, poems, songs, and filmstrips. She has also worked as a children's editor and a teacher of writing for children. She received a B.A. in English Literature from Park College, Parkville, Missouri, and an M.A. in Musicology from Indiana University. Ms. Greene lives in St. Louis, Missouri. When she isn't writing, she likes to read, travel, sing, do volunteer work at her church—and write some more. Her The Super Snoops and the Missing Sleepers *and* Sandra Day O'Connor, First Woman on the Supreme Court *have also been published by Childrens Press.*